# PERFECTIONEUR
## FROM WORKAHOLIC TO WELL-BALANCED

# PERFECTIONEUR
## FROM WORKAHOLIC TO WELL-BALANCED

*One therapist's guide to get you there*

FOREWORD BY MELISSA DASILVA

**KHARA CROSWAITE BRINDLE**

Copyright © 2020-2021 Khara Croswaite Brindle

All rights reserved. This book or any portion thereof may not be reproduced or used in any manner without the express written permission of the Publisher except for the use in brief quotations in a book review.

Printed by Amazon, in the United States.

First printing, 2020.

February 28, 2021

What if work is my self-care? This thought lodged in my mind in the first year of *Perfectioneur* being published. How could it not? This book was written and launched during a pandemic, which has stretched all of our abilities to take care of ourselves. Creativity is my outlet. Working keeps me grounded. *Success in the name of sanity.* It's a delicate dance where workaholism remains a challenge. I know from the mass of materials out there on burnout and workaholic culture that I'm not unique in this fight. I threw myself into it and celebrated *Perfectioneur* becoming an Amazon #1 Best Seller within it's first year! With each milestone, my workaholism crept back in. It was more subtle this time then bam! I found myself in the familiar pattern of no breaks in my calendar, working weekends, and coming home late. It was the perfect storm. It's also why I wanted to add to the book the two biggest challenges this first year has handed to me; watching my warning signs and saying no to more.

My hope is that you will surround yourself with like-minded entrepreneurs who can hold you accountable in your path of self-discovery. I know family and friends have been my saving grace in recovering from a second backslide into workaholism to again finding myself closer to well-balanced. That and revisiting the exercises in *Perfectioneur*, recognizing it will take more than one review to truly adopt these streamlined strategies as a driven professional. It's a conscious effort every day. You too can embrace the skills in this book and you don't have to do it alone. My greatest joy will be that you find the additions to the second edition of *Perfectioneur: From Workaholic to Well-Balanced* invaluable in crafting your own workaholism to wellness journey. Don't give up!

You are your own success story.

Warmly,
**Khara**

# SUCCESS ★ STORIES

Ok, aside from moving, traveling to foreign country and dealing with all of the little changes that come with both of those changes I have been struggling to keep up with work. Literally drowning in work.

One of my long term clients decided to do a whole new rebranding during all of my moving and they have just loaded more and more and more work on. In a project meeting with them last week the CEO mentioned that my work wasn't looking as creative as it could and asked if I needed a break from the project to rejuvenate. I had no idea that this was an option and was like a weight lifted off of my shoulders. He told me to think it over, come up with a plan where I can have a break, but still get it done by the end of the year.

So this morning I sat down to type out my plan for them and also included a list of things I need from them to make this happen. One of the items I mentioned was to focus on the top 3 projects and work to get those 100% done. Then work on the next 3 projects, etc... That way we are actually getting items done. I also emphasized that they couldn't add anything to the list until we got everything done. As I was proof reading the email I realized that that was one of the things you wrote about in your book--picking the top number of items on your to-do list and not adding anything to the list until those are done. I have been doing that in my personal life, but have been struggling with how to implement that with clients.

Just wanted to let you know how your book has helped me in my personal and professional life. Your book has important tools that I need to keep being productive and successful.

Thank you!
**Liv**

# SUCCESS ★ STORIES

I am emailing you to, first of all, thank you! Thank you for your passion, vulnerability, and shining your light through your book, "Perfectioneur!" It really helped me and others be able to shine our light and have difficult conversations with ourselves. Your book is an invitation to a functional analysis of the entrepreneur. It challenges us to ask about where we were, where we are, and where we aspire to be and what we want to become. Due to your writing and insights (personally and professionally), I have been able to address key points that have been life changing and also inspiring. I have been able to make a list of my pros and cons, priorities and challenges and as a result, I have made a decision to make a huge shift and change in my career. Again, all from your book (and workbook)!

As I discussed these changes with my spouse, I can't help but address the key points that hit home. I truly respect and honor the approach you took with validating the human in us as we develop professionally. Understanding the culture of busyness and how it has been implanted in us as a sign of self-worth and if not careful, can lead to our demise. This leads to ongoing need to set boundaries (I admit, this is the part I disliked you). I had to remind myself that boundaries are set not for rejection, but for protection. Protect me and others in their 5 domains (mental, emotional, physical, relational, and spiritual). Which slid into self-advocating for my needs and practicing more self-care within my 5 domains and become aware of the lack of movement somatically due to the ongoing charge (or analysis paralysis) that occurs when I get stuck in "the doings" of the entrepreneur rather than "the being" with myself and needs. Self-care is now in my planner under lunch, walk, stretch, etc. The awareness experience of confronting my inner saboteur was a real challenge that was needed and an ongoing challenge that I have taken on. In sharing with other colleagues, I realized this is leading to burn out and in some, compassion fatigue.

## SUCCESS ★ STORIES

Your experience in the dual role of entrepreneur (with expectations) and person (just being authentic self) shed light on the unspoken reality of the field and professionals. At times, as entrepreneurs we feel deflated, alone, and challenged with no one to talk to or rely on for support. Your experience reminds us to look within (soma, potential, psyche/soul, and skills) and take a time out, walk, meditate, breathe, stretch, re-focus, re-align, re-center, and most of all re-engage.

Khara, I can go on and on discussing the skills and the gifts that came through your book, but most of all, I'd rather share it, gift it and not only in English but also Spanish. As I move forward in my new adventures with Transcending Consulting Group as trainer and consultant to other clinicians (nationally and internationally), I will constantly be reminded that this new business and organization was a direct result of your book, Perfectioneur. Its challenges to be more aligned with my passion and re-aligned my to the course I was originally on. The tools, exercises, awareness experiences, and tasks are gifts that prepare us to shine, if we are up for the challenge.

Your book and you are truly a gift my friend!

Yours truly,
*J. Alex Castro*

# CONTENTS

**Foreword** ........................................................................... XI
Chapter 1 **Seeking Self Worth** .......................................... 1
Chapter 2 **What is a Perfectioneur?** ................................. 7
Chapter 3 **People Pleasers Unite** ..................................... 13
Chapter 4 **Burnout as a Snuffed Flame? It's a Forest Fire.** ... 17
Chapter 5 **The Power of Movement** ............................... 21
Chapter 6 **Remove the Badge of Busyness** .................... 25
Chapter 7 **Go Lean on Lists** ............................................ 29
Chapter 8 **Creating is Your Happy Place** ....................... 33
Chapter 9 **Stopping the Steamroll** .................................. 35
Chapter 10 **Give Up Control** ............................................ 39
Chapter 11 **Who's in Your Orbit?** .................................... 43
Chapter 12 **Accept Your Inner Boss Bitch** ...................... 47
Chapter 13 **Pick Your Power Words** ............................... 51
Chapter 14 **Avoid Setting Up Camp with Your Inner Critic** .. 53
Chapter 15 **Learning to Accept Compliments** ................ 57
Chapter 16 **Lean into Leadership** .................................... 61
Chapter 17 **The Power of Vulnerability** .......................... 63
Chapter 18 **Asking for Help** .............................................. 67
Chapter 19 **The Risk of Relapse** ....................................... 71
Chapter 20 **Rest Versus Restoration** ................................ 75
Chapter 21 **Watch Your Warning Signs** .......................... 79
Chapter 22 **Say Yes to No (More)!** ................................... 83
Chapter 23 **Find Your Voice** ............................................ 87
**Host a *Type A Soiree*** ....................................................... 91
**References** ......................................................................... 93

# FOREWORD
## By Melissa DaSilva, LICSW

I started my own business out of necessity, which is why a lot people take the terrifying leap into entrepreneurship. The only business experience I had before starting my practice was selling bikinis on the beach every summer while in high school. Building my own business from the ground up wasn't exactly my childhood dream, but if I could sell the most challenging piece of clothing to anyone, I knew I would be able to figure out how to run a successful business. Even then, the journey to create the business I wanted was long and difficult.

My goal was to create a business that addressed mental health issues in my community as well as provide jobs for clinicians that wanted a different experience. During that process, business became the focus of my life, and I soon learned that being a solo entrepreneur can easily be all-consuming, lonely, and emotionally draining. I loved learning all the aspects of creating a business. It was easy to find information on business practices, but my personal life suffered in the process.

It's hard for others to understand the isolation that can come with professional success. Through all my research in learning how to run a business, I hadn't come across any resource that addressed these specific issues, which made me feel like I must be the only one experiencing these feelings. That led to not disclosing my self-doubt and fears to anyone that could help.

Looking back, I wish that I had Khara Croswaite Brindle's book *Perfectioneur: From Workaholic to Well Balanced, One Therapist's Guide to Get You There* to guide me through the process. The emotions and experiences she describes in her book mirror mine perfectly, and it was comforting to be retroactively justified in my own feelings. Khara touches on all the struggles new therapists and entrepreneurs go through when branching out. Not only does she validate these experiences, she offers useful action plans at the end of each chapter as a way to overcome barriers to professional success and mental wellbeing. Anyone who reads this book will pick up life-changing advice and the support needed to be successful without having to sacrifice their mental health or personal life.

**Melissa DaSilva, LICSW**
*The Queer Career Coach*
Author and Entrepreneur

# 1
# SEEKING SELF WORTH

Psychology is all about exploring why people do what they do. Or that's at least the preface of PSY 101 Introduction to Psychology, a college class I love teaching that sparks young minds and their interest in emotions, behaviors, and thus, themselves. The same group of individuals who want to know if they can find happiness, joy, work-life balance, and purpose. Simon Sinek (2009) identifies this generation as wanting impact in their lives, being told they could be and do anything, and is a generation that lives in a world of instant gratification. The stereotyped Millennials, with both strengths and challenges. Depending on which research you reference, Millennials are roughly the generation born 1981 to 1996

(Debczak, 2019), which can be seen as a significant number of people. Dr. Jean Twenge (2017) describes the Millennial generation as having increased anxiety, depression, and job and relationship dissatisfaction. Amidst a mass of generalizations including ghosting, job hopping, and tons of drive, Millennials were at one point referred to as the therapy generation (Drexler, 2019), pursuing therapy to build meaningful connections, tackle dating dilemmas, and work on themselves through pursuit of meaningful careers and hobbies.

I too am a Millennial. An "Elder Millennial" according to comedienne Iliza Shlesinger (2018). As a therapist working with other young adults in this generation and Gen Z, I can't help but notice how our self-worth is wrapped up in what we do. In the therapy community, self-worth is best explored through messages and beliefs about ourselves. Exploring that messaging we received as children and how it shapes who we become. To do this, therapists have introduced a tree visual. The worries and anxieties initially presented in therapy or the elements we are consciously aware of are the leaves of the tree. Going deeper cognitively on what these thoughts say about us, we get to the trunk of the tree. And finally, going even deeper on what these thoughts say about us, we get to the roots of the tree, representing those negative core beliefs that drive our behaviors. I warn clients that when we find and uncover their negative core beliefs, a visceral reaction shows up in our bodies, including unpleasant sensations of nausea, throat tightness, avoidant eye contact, tears, anxiety, and other discomfort related to shame and vulnerability. Core beliefs can eventually be verbalized as "I am unlovable, I am unworthy, and I am a failure." Francine Shapiro's Eye Movement Desensitization and Reprocessing (EMDR) trauma protocol (2001) is a type of therapy that encourages clients to name and experience their negative core beliefs in order to successfully heal them. I myself believe that knowing your core beliefs allows

## CHAPTER 1 - SEEKING SELF WORTH

clarity in why you do what you do, what drives your behavior, and contributes to how you show up in this world.

So please allow me to practice the vulnerability of naming my self-worth as a Millennial, 30-something, driven and restless female therapist and entrepreneur. My negative core beliefs state that "I am only loveable for what I do for others." "My worth is in what I do for others." "I am only as good as what I do for others." Through countless leadership trainings and my own therapeutic work, it didn't take long to see these same themes showing up again and again. Does any of this sound familiar? Can you relate? If you have ever self-identified as a people person, a people-pleaser, a highly sensitive person (HSP), a helper or caregiver, your core beliefs could be similar. Don Richard Rison and Russ Hudson (1996) describe this as the cornerstone of an Enneagram Type 2 person, a personality test that highlights how we relate to others based on childhood experiences, traumas, and messages we received. As someone who's core beliefs say my worth is wrapped up in what I contribute, you can image how often my boundaries have been skewed and challenged by putting others' needs before my own.

I've found myself saying yes when I wanted to say no, saying yes out of obligation or fear of missed opportunities, saying yes to be liked, and helping others at the risk of resentment, burnout, and decline in my own health. I've pursued busyness to feel like I had purpose, thinking that if I was making progress on goals I'd set for myself, I would feel happy. Content. *Fulfilled.* I should mention I'm truly an Enneagram 3 wing 2. Meaning I also measure my success in what I accomplish in my life such as what's on my goal list, what's on my resume, and what accolades I receive. The Enneagram personality test (find your type at enneagraminstitute.com) was a turning point for me both personally and professionally. Finally! A personality profile that looks at how we relate to others! A test that takes the negative core beliefs that drive our behaviors and shows us warning signs of how we will look and present to others when unbalanced or unhealthy.

The Enneagram isn't for the faint of heart. In training, therapists were told that we'd know we'd identified the right type for ourselves when reading the list of weaknesses leads to feelings of nausea and mild mortification. Enter another visceral reaction of nausea, embarrassment, and shame. It happened to me. In a group of 20 therapists, I discovered my Enneagram type and felt pride in my strengths quickly squashed by shame in my weaknesses. Is that truly how I look to others? Is that how I want to show up? The truth, for myself and other young adults I've worked with, is that we want feedback and recognition to know we are doing alright in this world. The irony? We can't really sit with compliments when we receive them. It's uncomfortable. It can feel downright painful. Have you noticed? Perhaps you or someone you care about feels the same. We smile and say thank you and move on as quickly as we can. We don't let the compliment sink in and we don't allow ourselves to feel any of the pride, pleasure, or warm fuzzies that a genuine compliment can provide. We were taught to be humble. Don't let it go to your head! Don't be cocky! Don't brag, people won't like you. It has become a complicated dance for many of us to be equal parts present, authentic, vulnerable, humble, and confident. Explore taking up space, finding your voice, saying no. No is a complete sentence, I've heard. Yet for those of us whose self-worth is wrapped up in what we do, *no* is a hard sentence to practice.

Practice is important. Practice is key. Self-worth is at the root of why I currently identify as a Perfectioneur. A work in progress. You too can become a healthy Perfectioneur to live the life you've always wanted. This book is a journey about recognizing and embracing your Perfectioneur identity. Sitting with it. Getting to know it. Accepting its strengths. Learning how to overcome its unhealthy edges to embrace recovery, healing, and health. Are you ready to

## CHAPTER 1 - SEEKING SELF WORTH

jump in and achieve your work-life balance to be one step closer to fulfillment? Join me as we rewrite our self-worth story. It can be better than we've ever imagined.

# 2
# WHAT IS A PERFECTIONEUR?

*Perfectioneur* (French): Perfection.
   Control Freak
   Entrepreneur
   Workaholic
   Type A Personality
   Enneagram Type 3
   **Perfectioneur**

Perfectioneurs are *Perfectionist Entrepreneurs*. It's a term I woke up with at 4am one morning, a week before my birthday. I discovered it was another way of describing who I am in the world of business. As a therapist entrepreneur. *How I show up*. My brain exploded with the possibilities! I coined the term Perfectioneur, first in my social circles and then beyond with fellow entrepreneurs. With excitement and anxiety, I pitched it to a group of business women to see what they thought. They chuckled. They reflected. They related! Relating by realizing that Perfectioneurs are the only ones standing in our own way. Naming that our pursuit of perfection prevents progress and invites in *analysis paralysis*. Recognizing that we can make ourselves sick in our efforts to succeed.

Have you ever worked so hard at something that you made yourself sick? Maybe it was that time at the gym where you pushed yourself so hard in a workout that you felt physically ill. Or during dead week in college, that week before finals? Where you worked so hard to feel prepared, only to get sick after finals were over. Working so hard to master something, it's something I know a lot about as a Perfectioneur.

Perfectioneurs are a new breed of entrepreneurs. We embody the American dream of hustling hard to make an impact. We work long hours, weekends, and the early hours of the morning. We get creative inspiration at 4am and can't go back to sleep. We are happiest when creating, building, and changing things for the better. Perfectioneurs have the drive of other entrepreneurs, with a big helping of perfectionism, a generous scoop of self-criticism, a cup of imposter syndrome, and a dash of poor boundaries. Perfectioneurs are at risk of working so hard that they make themselves sick. Ignoring the warning signs of burnout, fatigue, and eventual mental break or collapse, Perfectioneurs are internally motivated to keep going, not only from a place of measuring self-worth, but to help others, to make an impact, and to leave their mark.

I should know. As a driven Perfectioneur, I ran myself into the ground to succeed. *To conquer or die*. A family motto I believe to my core, even going so far as to tattoo it on my body. I almost

## CHAPTER 2 - WHAT IS A PERFECTIONEUR?

lost everything I worked hard for as the result. In one critical moment, I was sitting in a college classroom after a long day of work, trying to learn more about the nonprofit sector when my future wellness coach was invited in as a guest speaker. Finding myself puffy, pale, and emotionally exhausted, her words and presence stirred something in me. She spoke of self-care being pushed in our industry in ways she couldn't embrace. It was something I could relate to because frankly, I couldn't connect with colleagues who said self-care was easy, effortless, and worthwhile either. I needed someone who could look me in the eye and say I was on the fast track to collapse. That my relationships were suffering. That I was exacerbating the autoimmune condition I was diagnosed with two years before. Through missteps and hard work, I got to the place where I could truly hear it from my coach. *Eventually.* Moving from contemplation to preparation and finally action. It took years of hearing concern from others, but I didn't let it sink in. In my stubbornness, I could have ignored the hair loss, eczema outbreaks, weight gain, and fatigue. I could have handled seeing my swollen face and limbs in the mirror on random days of the week. I told myself I *chose* to work holidays and weekends, the week between my marriage and my honeymoon, and weeks when I was scheduled to visit family. I had worked hard to recognize my *need to be needed*. I was trying my best to ignore the mood swings where I'd wake up almost daily not wanting to get out of bed, instead fantasizing about getting rid of my businesses, getting on a plane, running away, and starting over. The feelings of dread were overwhelming and I was making it work. I was surviving. But surviving wasn't enough. What really pushed healing into a top priority for me was my spouse.

My loving, easy-going, and patient spouse. He'd put up with the mood swings and the catastrophic thinking as I tried to make an impact. He handled my starting work at 6am and coming home at almost 9pm every night, drained of any small talk or energy to connect. He showed patience as I texted him in my panic to escape, start over, leave town. He understood that I wanted to feel in control of my life and supported me as I tried different tactics to make it happen. Until one day, as I was inhaling my late night dinner on the couch next to him—him having eaten at a normal time—he asked if my future plans included changing my work hours. He stated he missed seeing me and was sad to see me only an hour a day. *That's 7 hours a week*. Now that might not feel that alarming to you as the reader. He did in fact ask it calmly and quietly without judgement. But for anyone who's met him, they know for him to voice a concern at all, it's been festering in silence for a while. For months most likely. My spouse doesn't ask for much, and him deciding to address my lack of presence in the relationship both physically and emotionally was a big deal. A big enough deal that I lost my appetite instantly as panic took the place of food in my now hollow stomach. It was speaking volumes to the unhappiness in our relationship. The fast approaching train of doom and gloom in my mind was screaming I was going to lose him. Luckily, the universe didn't want this to happen and neither did I. I'd just met a professional the week before that could help me. My spouse's question was the finally kick in the ass I needed. So the next day I scheduled a consultation with the coach I'd seen talk so honestly, the one who said self-care isn't easy, and tearfully told her I needed help because I didn't want to lose my spouse, my love, my glue.

Isn't that funny? Not ha-ha funny but painful funny. It took the potential of losing someone I care about to kick my butt into gear. Not my own rapid emotional and physical decline. Not the mood swings that were excruciating to experience. Not the burn-out with my therapy clients. The element that finally got me out of my stubborn denial and into action was the implied loss of the relationship that keeps me going. For most Perfectioneurs I've connected with, relationships are in fact the buffer that keep them actively pursuing work-life balance. If we can't do it for ourselves, we try to do it for others.

# 3
# PEOPLE PLEASERS UNITE

Doing things for others is not a foreign concept for Perfectioneurs. It's one of the primary drivers for what we do and why we do it. Perfectioneurs have those core beliefs that tie their value into what they do for others. In my worse moments of running myself into the ground, I was saying yes to requests, questions, opportunities, and demands from my work community and ignoring the requests, questions, and softer demands of my personal relationships. My personal relationships weren't seeing me at all. My family felt like I was avoiding them, and in some form, I was. My spouse was getting the remaining energy I had left after work, which I have to admit wasn't much. I found small talk and socializing to be exhausting and later recognized I was actively avoiding scheduling it in my calendar.

Instead, I got wrapped up in my performance and worth through work demands. Were my clients getting their needs met? Was I helping them heal? Should I assist that colleague so that I can keep the door open to opportunities later? Do I say yes to coffee with another therapist I don't know so they can "pick my brain?" Do I respond to these emails asking me for advice, information, and referrals because they assume being as connected to the community as I am, that I have all the answers? As you can imagine, this made my work life even more full. So it was no wonder I came home empty every night, devoid of connection or grace for my spouse including his wants and needs.

Can you relate to the demands of work leaving you a shell of yourself for homelife or socializing? Perfectioneurs, as driving forces, will say yes to keep momentum going. Yes to creativity. Yes to opportunity. Yes to collaboration. Each yes comes at a cost. Costs of energy, time, resources, time off, socializing, libido, and sense of humor. Perhaps you've noticed how your boundaries have skewed. For many of us, it's the resentment and overwhelm that show up when we get another request, demand, or question we didn't account for in our overly-packed schedule. I'm talking about the epic meltdowns when your car gets a flat tire while you are on your way to work, when your kid leaves crumbs on the kitchen counter, and when your spouse forgets to grab milk at the store. These big energy outbursts that overwhelm your already exhausted system and are really displaced burnout. You aren't resentful and angry at the family per se, you are angry that, in a state of overwhelm and being overworked, you feel the demands keep coming. Can't others see you are *overwhelmed?*

You would think so, but even as I moved closer and closer to meltdown status, my colleagues, friends, and family weren't always

## CHAPTER 3 - PEOPLE PLEASERS UNITE

aware of my state of mind. Perfectioneurs are all about productivity and impact remember? So even as I was waging war with my emotions every morning, clients, colleagues, and the community at large saw me kicking ass and taking names. Maybe you too, are good at hiding how you truly feel. Maybe you too thought the badge of busyness would keep you from realizing how unhappy you are in your current circumstance. Or maybe, like me, it took attending a training to realize you are officially in burnout.

# 4
# BURNOUT AS A SNUFFED FLAME? IT'S A FOREST FIRE.

I got tired of saying yes and feeling resentful as I said it. I was tired of having what I like to call 'adult tantrums' by myself or in front of my spouse. I was done with being negative. I became a shell of myself, sticking to survival mode. I couldn't laugh at funny things and I couldn't feel much but fatigue and a sense of scorn. Being a therapist as well as an entrepreneur, I'd heard whispers of burnout, compassion fatigue, and vicarious trauma. Being four years into community mental health and my career at the time, I was wondering if I was suffering from any or all three.

Burnout for so many entrepreneurs, small business owners, and professional helpers can be described as fatigue, fluctuating motivation, low mood, high anxiety, and a jaded lens from which to view the world, to name a few. Laura van Dermoot Lipsky and Connie Burk (2009) name it beautifully in their book *Trauma Stewardship*. Additionally, attending a training on vicarious trauma brought a lot of things to light for me, including warning signs of burnout that were personalized to me and ideas for how to cope and change. The imagery people use for burnout tends to be a match or flame that's been extinguished or snuffed out. For me, my burnout felt like a raging forest fire, emotions out of control and consuming all areas of my life. Leaving wreckage in its wake. I was judgmental, irritable, and cynical when not in therapist mode. My anger that masked unhappiness would lash out at my family and contribute to elevated road rage. My anxiety and thus, my controlling tendencies were skyrocketing daily. I found myself fixating on certain things and resenting others for not working the fast-paced timelines I'd set in my head. I found myself micromanaging others to feel a sense of control. I found my pleasantries and greetings absent in emails, leaving abrupt sentences that sounded like demands instead. In a nutshell, I see now that I wasn't the most pleasant person to be around back then.

In fact, Perfectioneurs are at higher risk of not only trying to control people, places, and things, they are at greater risk of steamrolling others in their vision to make an impact, achieve results, and gain momentum. What does steamrolling look like? "You're either with me, or get out of my way." *My way or the highway* on steroids. Rolling right over you as an inconvenience if you aren't unified or contributing to the vision. Plowing ahead with limited regard for your feelings or needs. Increased control and resentment that you can't show up at the same speed, level of commitment, or productivity the Perfectioneur expects. As you can imagine, this doesn't bode well for connecting with others. It can be quite lonely. Thus, relationships are the primary thing to suffer outside of physical health decline for unhealthy Perfectioneurs.

## CHAPTER 4 - BURNOUT AS A SNUFFED FLAME? IT'S A FOREST FIRE.

If this sounds like you, there's hope! You don't have to feel like you must hop on a plane and start over somewhere else. You don't have to feel the heaviness of burnout and fatigue forever. Yes, entrepreneurs are at higher risk of mental health challenges including depression, ADHD, and substance use (Freeman, 2015). Yes, Perfectioneurs and entrepreneurs struggle with work-life balance. Yes, we have some work to do on setting realistic expectations for ourselves and others. Just imagine channeling your creative energy and drive to pursuing health and wellness. How successful could it feel to put as much energy into our health and relationships as we do our business goals? Talk about results! Join me on the journey to health and healing with some concrete tools that can help you feel one step closer to work-life balance and satisfaction.

# 5
# THE POWER OF MOVEMENT

I remember the first homework my coach gave me was ten minutes of walking outside a day. It sounds simple doesn't it? She loves to remind me how resistant I was to it at first. My excuses? *I'm too busy*. I need to answer emails. I need to eat something super-fast before jumping back into the work. I need to whittle down my to-do list. She pointed out that I already knew the benefits of movement as a therapist. As someone who worked with a lot of clients with anxiety, I can recognize the importance of movement to work some of the tension out of the body, to feel more grounded, and to not have anxiety fester or become increasingly unmanageable. Not to mention the clarity of thoughts that happen when we engage in walking and other bilateral movements. So why couldn't I do it?

*I don't have time.* That was the predominant thought. It took some effort on my part to carve out time for movement. At first it took a pop up reminder on my phone to keep it in the forefront of my mind during each jam-packed day. I started with getting up and stretching. Then it evolved into carving out a lunch hour in my calendar that included eating and a short walk. Right? *Time to eat. On the calendar.* Then it moved to parking further away from the store or errand so I'd be forced to walk a bit more. The magic? The more I walked outside, the better I felt! I was taking deeper, restorative breaths. I was feeling more alert and appreciative of my body. I was navigating the sugar slumps and sleepiness after lunch. I was feeling joy in being outside. Before I knew it, I was looking forward to walking each day. Walking to work, walking for errands, walking with my spouse in the evenings as we checked in with one another. Walking to the grocery store on weekends. Walking to cope with anger, restlessness, boredom and lethargy when my body went from a million miles an hour to having some down time on a Sunday. It was sneaky. It was subtle. Walking went from being a chore to a go-to coping skill and necessary part of my day, every day.

How can you start? Maybe it's getting up every hour to stretch, drink water, and stand to allow circulation and flow within your body. Maybe it's pausing before you leave your car to walk into work, noticing your steps, surroundings, and nature in a brief practice of mindfulness. Or if you're like me, you have to schedule it or it doesn't happen. Old-school planners are making a comeback in the battle of work-life balance. Perhaps you invest in one and block out time for movement and see how it goes. Finding an accountability buddy, someone who can walk with you or at least ask you about it, can be a great motivator to get it done. Lastly, making walks part of your work routine such as lunch breaks or walking to work if possible can shift thinking from walking being an inconvenience or luxury for free time only to walking being a part of a schedule or plan. Transforming movement into an important, low-energy task with high-energy benefits.

## *Perfectioneur Pointers*: MAKING TIME FOR MOVEMENT

- ★ Start with stretching.

- ★ Utilize a planner or personal fitness device to remind you to move daily.

- ★ Park farther away to get more steps.

# 6
# REMOVE THE BADGE OF BUSYNESS

Part of the success of incorporating movement into your daily routine is addressing the American culture of busyness. Otherwise when will you find the time? Consider how you respond to the ever-present question, "how are you?"

> How are you?
> Busy!
> How's work?
> *So busy!*

For many Americans, busyness is the norm. It's an expectation to be busy in order to make meaningful things happen. It's the go-

go-go mentality where one is supposed to feel guilty if they take a vacation or relax on the weekends. Brené Brown (2015) points out that it doesn't actually serve us to wear the badge of busyness. As a therapist, I see patterns of behavior that reinforce remaining busy for all sorts of reasons. Perhaps there is an illusion of progress in staying busy. Some people stay busy to avoid the deeper emotions they don't want to feel. They may have the thought, "if I stay busy, I won't have to feel the unhappiness/discontent/fear in my life." For mental health professionals, the joke is that we like to focus on others so we don't have to think about our own problems.

I'm guilty of this as a therapist. When things were getting rocky in my personal life, I'd throw myself into work and focus on others with joy! Hurray, I can stop thinking about my life! Hurray for the distraction! With gratitude I would immerse myself in other things, giving my mind a break from the self-criticism and ever-present scrutiny. I realized when I finished something, I'd add something back onto my schedule to keep the same level of busyness. The same level of high energy and illusion of momentum. I would panic in seeing blank space in my day. It took my coach asking the hard questions about how fulfilled and content I was in the busyness to realize how miserable I felt. To realize I was spinning my wheels and burning out. It was a painful process, recognizing that busyness wasn't serving me. Yet it was worthwhile because as soon as I could admit I was dissatisfied with certain parts of my life and was tired of spinning out, I could begin the practice of channeling my focus to finding solutions.

Do you find yourself struggling with negative thoughts and unhappiness when you are alone? Does your mood plummet when there is down time in your schedule you didn't expect? Maybe during the late hours at night when distractions are few and far between? If so, you are not alone. Perfectioneurs have been there and it isn't pleasant. Would you like to feel more content? Fulfilled? Like you

### CHAPTER 6 - REMOVE THE BADGE OF BUSYNESS

have a purpose? Ask yourself if you are taking on new tasks or projects out of a desire to remain busy and fight boredom. Do the tasks actually resonate with your bigger goals? Do they keep you feeling like you are in momentum? Or are they just busy work? Be honest with yourself. Getting in touch with down time to think and create could be a vital step to uncovering the answers you seek about change for the better. After all, no one likes to feel like a hamster on a wheel.

## *Perfectioneur Pointers*: BUSTING BUSYNESS

- ★ Allow down time for creativity.

- ★ Ask yourself, am I doing this to remain busy? Does this align with my goals?

- ★ Are you feeling busy or bored? Find ways to take your hamster off the wheel.

# 7
# GO LEAN ON LISTS

Taking inventory of your priorities and exploring the purpose of the work in order to remove busyness is an important step of going lean on your to-do list. It's led to worldwide exploration into 4-day work schedules and concepts like Tim Ferris' *4-hour work week*. In the therapeutic community, it is recommended that individuals keep their daily lists at no more than seven items or goals per day. Why? Because our memories can only hold so many tasks without chunking them, a memorizing technique we see for phone numbers, addresses, and more. What are the benefits of a lean list? We know that we can multitask, but with limited energy towards each item. Therefore multitasking can be done, but at what cost? Can you remember your seven (or fewer) tasks each day? Are they memorable day to day, week to week?

## Here's an activity to put this in context:

**Step 1:** Think about all the things you want to accomplish in the next six months, both personally and professionally. Write them all down.

**Step 2:** Take that list you've created and circle your top ten priorities. Do these ten items feel most important right now?

**Step 3:** What if I told you that all the remaining items have to be ignored? That you can't work on them until these top 10 priorities, deemed most important, are accomplished in the next 6 months?

If you are like me, you had some anxiety creep up immediately. Perhaps you felt tricked, betrayed, and irritated like I did when I completed this activity for the first time. To be told I had to ignore the other goals for my top 10 felt uncomfortable and unfair. I found myself trying to negotiate and convince my coach that I could do it all. *Typical Perfectioneur.* She held firm, emphasizing the importance of creative energy being focused on the tasks at hand, allowing it to feel more like progress being made versus the hamster on the wheel feeling. So I decided to give it a chance. Do you know what happened? I felt more alert, clear, and productive when focusing on my top 10. As a Perfectioneur, I felt in control when telling myself to put other goals to the side until these were accomplished. I felt it was easier to say no to other tasks, requests, and busy work in wanting to keep my focus. I also felt reassured that the additional goals would get attention as soon as I finished my top 10, writing them down so as not to forget about them for another time.

Yes, it starts off as uncomfortable, with a lot of resistance and irritation. Perhaps you feel similarly, thinking to yourself, "no thanks,

## CHAPTER 7 - GO LEAN ON LISTS

no one can tell me what to do!" Here's the beauty of it. *You get to decide.* You get to decide which 10 goals are the top 10. You get to decide if and when they are finished. You get to decide when to take something else on in its place to keep progress and momentum going. As a recovering Perfectioneur, I can speak to the freedom and excitement of seeing things progress more quickly because I've carved out time and energy just for them. I am no longer being pulled in 12 million directions. I am no longer distracted by items that weren't a priority. I no longer struggle with saying no. I get to decide my top priorities, and so do you.

### *Perfectioneur Pointers:* GO LEAN, NOT LONG

- ★ Complete the activity above and stick with your top 10.

- ★ Ask yourself, does the task at hand connect back to my top 10 goals? If not, put it off until one of the top 10 is completed.

- ★ Thought reframe: It's not telling you what to do, it's helping you focus.

# 8
# CREATING IS YOUR HAPPY PLACE

Permitting yourself to focus on your top priorities frees up valuable time for work-life balance and creativity. As an entrepreneur, you function best when creating. I'm not talking arts and crafts, although those can be fun. I'm talking about creating something new, something that can make a difference or an impact in your work, homelife, or the world at large. The same is true for Perfectioneurs. Perfectioneurs have an aversion to feeling stagnant, stuck, and unchanged. Therefore they are happiest when given opportunities to create.

In my case, I saw myself evolve from believing myself a closer, a finisher, a person who gets things done, to a starter or person who gets an idea or concept up and running and then passes the torch to someone else to maintain it. I didn't realize that what I was doing could be considered the definition of a serial entrepreneur. At that point in my life, I didn't consider myself an entrepreneur at all. I thought I was just looking to diversify my income stream with new projects. Yet creating is the essence of entrepreneurs. Words to describe them include innovative, dynamic, thought-leaders, and passionate catalysts of change. I know these words spoke to me as a blossoming entrepreneur, changing the way I saw myself as I created and pursued new opportunities.

What supports creation for you? When you think back to your happiest moments, what do they entail? Some businesses recognize the importance of creative space, identifying 20% of the workweek for employees to focus on a work-related project of their choice (Grant, 2017). The results? Creation of some of the newest ideas for business improvement, products or content development, not to mention employees feel more emotionally invested in the company (Grant, 2017). For so many Perfectioneurs, they are happiest in moments of significant momentum, constant creativity, and when they are kicking ass at their goals. The closer we get to feeling fulfilled while honoring our drive and purpose, the more motivated we become!

## *Perfectioneur Pointers*: CREATING IS KEY

- ★ Identify your areas of creativity. What do you like to do?

- ★ Explore how you can carve out time for creativity each week.

- ★ Imagine how 20% of your work week could look on the calendar to support time for creativity.

# 9
# STOPPING THE STEAMROLL

Once Perfectioneurs find their momentum and time for creativity, they are at risk of accelerating so fast that self-care and work-life balance are left in the dust. It is part of the equation of why a Perfectioneur moves into unhealthy space that warrants recovery. Yes, we've removed the badge of busyness to focus on tasks and goals that feel like top priorities. Yes, we've carved out time in our schedules for movement and creativity. What happens when we reach these goals? When we cross off our top 10 priorities, marking them as accomplished in 6 months or less? The hope is that we feel some sense of the pride and pleasure in accomplishing our goals. The pleasant sensations that come from progress and purpose. Some call it "stopping to smell the roses." Therapists name the desire to notice and experience our surroundings as mindfulness.

I've warned you that therapists make for their own worst clients and I am no exception. I can teach mindfulness to others no problem. I can speak to the importance of celebrating their strengths. But I'm bad at it for myself. One of my favorite moments in the therapeutic process is taking clients on a journey from start to finish when they are graduating from services. They've completed their goals and are preparing to close out from sessions. 9 times out of 10, they can't fully recall what they were like at the beginning of therapy when asked. It's as if their mind has created a mental block to protect them from the pain, grief, depression, or anxiety that catapulted them into the office in the first place. And yet, there is something so powerful about revisiting their former self and celebrating all they have accomplished. To see the before and after. To revel in the bright spots of achievement and growth. It's a privilege to be a part of that with them. It's my favorite part of graduation.

When it came to my own work and accomplishments, I too had a mental block. My mind would say, "next thing, next thing." Steamrolling ahead to the next goal. I was not celebrating my successes, sitting with my growth, or being mindful in any way. I was not giving myself kudos, pats on the back, or any other reward for a job well done. In fact, as a true Perfectioneur, I just expected that I should accomplish the things on my list, not as victories worth celebrating, but from a place of the "shoulds." I *should* make that growth in my business. I *should* be able to write 10 blogs in four weeks. I *should* launch an online class in two months. My clients who are closet Perfectioneurs have a similar dialogue. For some, it is physically painful to slow down and celebrate their successes. To invite in celebration is quickly followed by uninvited criticism. Worries that they are being cocky, full of themselves, or narcissistic in owning their accomplishments. Superstitions that something bad will happen if they voice their victories.

Have you struggled with celebrating your successes? Practicing mindfulness? Feeling motivated? Stopping to smell the roses reinforces positive behavior such as working hard to meet a deadline, returning a difficult phone call, or receiving constructive feedback at work. It contributes to finding the motivation to keep going. Another personal revelation? Being told that motivation is an emotion. *It fluctuates*. It comes and goes just like any other emotion. What powerful permission this is for Perfectioneurs to slow down and recognize the moments that matter, all from the place of keeping motivation and mood healthy and strong.

## *Perfectioneur Pointers:* BEING MINDFUL MATTERS

- ★ Identify one way you practice mindfulness.
- ★ Reflect on your self-talk. What are your 'shoulds?'
- ★ List some examples of internal motivators vs. external motivators for yourself.

# 10
# GIVE UP CONTROL

Stopping the steamroll to experience mindfulness and motivation is an important element of being a balanced Perfectioneur. Another vital component is giving up control. That's right. I just announced to the go-getter, Type A, perfectionists that they will have to give up control. *What?!* Perhaps you were just flooded with adrenaline hearing that? Panic? Outrage? Allow me to explain.

Perfectioneurs, like any other entrepreneur, have a vision for what they want. They have a plan and steps to get there. For many, the plan is to work long hours, sacrifice self-care, and hustle hard until they see results. Not surprisingly, they are putting it together on their own, as a one-person show which increases their risk for burnout. As the creative person with the vision, giving up some control could be the answer to finding time for meaningful ideas to take shape. Delegating tasks and asking for help could be important steps to giving up control and getting out of our own way.

As a self-identified control freak, this was a hard lesson to learn. I was used to working 3-5 jobs at a time, sacrificing time and energy to keep it all afloat. Bordering on burnout, I knew I had to do something different, but the thoughts of having to train someone to do some of the tasks I was completing each week was a huge deterrent. Especially when thoughts of self-sufficiency and reducing costs show up. "If I want something done right, I have to do it myself." "They will be slower to onboard and cost more money, so I might as well do it myself." Yes, as entrepreneurs sometimes we are bootstrapping things together to make them work. Yet the energy we are contributing to the tasks could be better served elsewhere, encouraging us to identify and delegate certain tasks to allow for greater focus and productivity.

## Here's an activity to explore the value of tasks even further:

**Step 1:** Identify and write down your daily tasks. Make a second list of weekly tasks that are your responsibility.

**Step 2:** Rank each of the identified tasks on a scale of 1-10 where 1 is *never enjoy it* and 10 is *always enjoy it*.

**Step 3:** Star or highlight tasks with a ranking of 6 and above. These tasks are identified as still worth doing in that they bring you some positive emotion and satisfaction more days than not.

**Step 4:** Circle tasks with a ranking of 5 and below. These tasks are worth exploring elimination, delegation, or assignment to third parties since you receive minimal to no enjoyment in completing them.

## CHAPTER 10 - GIVE UP CONTROL

**Step 5:** Identify next steps to reassigning tasks ranked 5 and under with a measurable plan and concrete timeline. Which are easiest to delegate? Which are the greatest priority when finding solutions?

If you're like me, it became pretty clear through this exercise which tasks were satisfying and which felt uninspiring and mundane. For me, the monotonous tasks of admin were targeted for reassignment in that they brought me no joy and prevented energy from being allotted for creative freedom and travel, two things that were of higher priority to me in my business and identity as a Perfectioneur. Another aha moment for me was having it named that influential individuals also delegate tasks and give up control to trusted persons to allow them to continue in their visionary work. "Khara," my coach said, "do you really think leaders want to spend their time doing laundry or running their billing each week? They hire other people to do that so they can put their creative energy elsewhere."

Therefore giving up control doesn't have to mean giving up *full* control. It means allowing for trusted people to help you and/or hiring a team of respected professionals to support your business as a well-oiled machine. Most importantly, as an entrepreneur, it is critical that your business run smoothly without you being present. This speaks to your ability to travel, work on other pursuits, and remain in a leadership role from afar while the business still benefits from your creative ideas and collaboration with your team. An appealing proposal for Perfectioneurs, wouldn't you say?

## *Perfectioneur Pointers*: TASKS AS A TEAM EFFORT

- ★ Complete the activity above. What tasks bring you joy and which could be reassigned?

- ★ Control doesn't mean you need to micromanage your business. Build a trusted team to run it.

★ Creative energy and ideas are easier to maintain when you aren't bogged down by the listless and mundane.

# 11
# WHO'S IN YOUR ORBIT?

We've talked about the importance of teams and trusted professionals to take the monotonous and mundane off your plate as a Perfectioneur. Identifying the trusted people in your circle you can call upon to help create results. Another question to ask yourself is, "who's in my orbit?" Who do you surround yourself with and why? Have you ever noticed how you feel after speaking with someone who operates from a negative lens? Perhaps someone who complains frequently? Someone who voices their unhappiness a lot? The 'Eeyores' of the world. Most likely, your energy was negatively impacted in some way. If you were healthy at the time, perhaps you noticed it and sent it back, like returning a volley in tennis. Notice the ball, connect with the ball, return the ball. Notice the energy, connect/observe the energy, return the energy. If you are feeling fatigued, burnt out, or otherwise exhausted, you might not notice the signs of their negativity and its impact on you so easily. Emotions of sadness, anger, fear, and negativity are all considered contagious.

Contagious and normed. Think of the water cooler that used to be the gathering place in an office. People would bond together, complaining about their horrible boss, long hours, or lack of snacks in the break room. Before you know it, everyone is adopting the same speaking style to connect each day. You bond with me by complaining about something I can agree with. You've become someone I can relate to. Then the negatively travels with you into your personal relationships where, in its worst form, it repels people from you in feeling like you are too negative or heavy to be around. *Ouch*. This is the importance of boundaries. Allowing ourselves to notice someone's discomfort or distress without absorbing it as our own. Boundaries in all relationships including the therapeutic relationship, where it is essential to still hold unconditional positive regard for someone who is suffering. Thus noticing how their pain and suffering has impacted their ability to connect with others without absorbing it into every fiber of our being.

Boundaries are easier said than done when in an unhealthy place. As an unwell Perfectioneur, I found myself experiencing the negative in my own life and trying to hold the negative for others in my therapeutic space. I discovered I was a shell of myself with low tolerance for complaints outside of the office. I was accused by loved ones of being mean, judgmental, and intolerant of change in my personal life. I was a negative, jaded, critical person to everyone but my clients. Strange how I compartmentalized that don't you think? I had to ask myself, who's in my orbit and do I want them to be there? In other words, I might not be able to control how many clients come in with negative viewpoints each week as the result of their trauma, but I could control who I surrounded myself with during the rest of the week.

Think about your personal and professional relationships. Your coworkers, your mentors, your peers. Your family, your friends, your intimate partner or spouse. Identify the individuals that energize you. Who light you up, animate, and inspire you. The people who, when you spend time with them, make you smile, laugh, and find yourself fully present and authentically yourself. These are the people to make time for in your busy schedule. These are the individuals to connect with on a regular basis as a creative entrepreneur.

In contrast, who are the people who drain you? Where time with them feels agonizingly slow. Where you feel fatigued or resentful because you had to work so hard in the relationship or conversation, gaining minimal reciprocity or meaningful return. These are the individuals who only reach out to you when they need something. They want to 'pick your brain' for their own gain. These are the people you will want to consider reducing contact with in order to protect your energy and your boundaries. I recognize it may be easier said than done if the individual is part of your family where contact is imminent or expected. You may have to reinforce boundaries by having a time limit on an interaction or by scheduling something restorative after the fact to replace the energy that you lost. As a Perfectioneur meeting tons of people and working your magic in business and goals, having some control over who you spend time with can be a crucial element of boundaries and burnout prevention.

## *Perfectioneur Pointers*: BUILDING BOUNDARIES

★ Ask yourself, "who's in my orbit?" How do these relationships serve me?

- ★ Identify relationships that energize you and schedule time for them.
- ★ Identify relationships that drain you and learn to limit them.

# 12
# ACCEPT YOUR INNER BOSS BITCH

By building and reinforcing boundaries as a healthy Perfectioneur, you may also have to accept your inner boss bitch to maintain those boundaries. I mentioned earlier that for me, I'm driven to say yes to others' requests out of a desire to be liked or a worry about missing an opportunity if I say no. As a woman, I also have to be mindful about coming across as aggressive or bitchy in my communication when saying no. My coach, in her matter of fact way, has reminded me that I can't control what other people think of me. Neither can you.

What would it be like to embrace the part of us that is labeled as an inner boss bitch? The part of us that could be better described as assertive, confident, self-assured, and driven. Perfectioneurs, in their perfectionist tendencies, can show up as uncooperative or aggressive when in an unhealthy state. We are at risk of steamrolling people, ignoring connection, and changing up agendas to suit our needs. We say "it's my way or get out of the way." We can be devoid of emotion or come across as insensitive when caught up in a deadline. Painting a picture of Perfectioneurs in our worst form.

Feeling your worst may be the catalyst for seeking therapy to work towards something better. Learning to reframe thoughts, feelings, and behaviors from a different viewpoint in order to pursue the changes you seek. I modeled reframing earlier by naming our inner boss bitch as assertive, confident, self-assured, and driven. Working towards being respected over being liked. A second goal of therapy could be to better understand patterns that show up. Patterns of healthy behaviors like working out, getting enough sleep, and having empathy for others. Identifying unhealthy patterns such as trying to control situations, fixating on things, lacking compassion, and forgoing sleep and exercise for projects. Is your inner boss bitch showing up a cue to step back and revaluate? Is it a warning sign that you need something? Is it a clue to boundaries being overstepped or broken?

As a healing Perfectioneur, I know my inner boss bitch being present is a sign that my boundaries are being tested or broken. She shows up when I feel resentful or taken advantage of by others. She voices outrage when I'm asked to do *one more thing* in a long list of to-dos when already feeling overwhelmed. She is responsible for the lack of pleasantries in my emails and a demanding tone to get things done that reduces the anxiety I feel. Recognizing her presence and my desire to control others are key warning signs for taking a different action, pivoting towards healthier shifts in my routine that bring me back to baseline and make me more pleasant to be around.

Accept your inner boss bitch as a sign of something deeper, allowing you to do the meaningful work of understanding the purpose,

### CHAPTER 12 - ACCEPT YOUR INNER BOSS BITCH

agenda, and patterns experienced when they show up. As a successful entrepreneur, more and more people will start asking things of you. This increases the importance of practicing saying *no* and preparing for any consequences that result. Reframe your inner boss bitch as the protector that they are. They may just save you from being overextended, overwhelmed, unfocused, and overworked as you work hard to achieve your work-life balance!

## *Perfectioneur Pointers*: INNER BOSS BITCH INSIGHTS

- ★ Be curious about when your inner boss bitch shows up. What does it mean for you?

- ★ How can your inner boss bitch be reframed into self-awareness statements? Finish this sentence: When my inner boss bitch shows up, I am…(exercising my boundaries, saying no, showing I'm overwhelmed).

- ★ What physical, emotional, and relational boundaries need to be in place to prevent your inner boss bitch from becoming overly reactive to others?

# 13
# PICK YOUR POWER WORDS

By engaging in positive reframes and embracing the importance of your inner boss bitch, it can feel like we've gained back personal power and self-control. With the desire for increased self-assurance, power words and the concept of manifestation might be worth checking out. Manifesting good things or thoughts is not a new concept. It shows up in the popular book *The Secret* by Rhonda Byrne (2007). It makes itself know through *Tarot* and voicing our intentions. Much like keeping focused, having power words that embody our values or goals can be a helpful tool in keeping ourselves on track and balanced as Perfectioneurs.

This may sound a bit whoo-whoo, even for a cognitive-behavioral therapist. Yet I've seen for myself and my clients the power of voicing hopes, dreams, and desires out loud. The connection to emotion when hearing your own voice, the reaction in the body, and the accountability of sharing it with others can have a positive effect on goal progression. If the negative cognitions related to self-worth have such visceral power over us, why can't the positive thoughts have a meaningful impact as well?

When starting my journey to become a healthier Perfectioneur, my power words were *focus* and *balance*. In year two of my journey, the words evolved into *confidence* and *richness*. Which words resonate for you? When you think of 1-3 key words that embody your vision and goals for the month, quarter, or year, what comes to mind?

## One Step Further!

Take this mental exercise a step further and find a local candle making shop or candle making kit to do at home. Identify scents that represent your power words and make a custom candle that you can light when wanting to invite in or manifest good energy, thoughts, and your power words. Have a time crunch or can't find a candle shop? Go to your natural grocery store and work your way through the essential oils section, picking 1-2 scents that embody your power words that you can use at home in a diffuser if you like.

### *Perfectioneur Pointers:* FROM WHOO-WHOO TO WHOO-HOO!

- ★ Discover your power words for this month, quarter, or year.

- ★ Practice writing, saying, or sharing your power words to reinforce them.

- ★ Take it one step further and create a custom candle with scents that represent your power words. Breathe them in.

# 14
# AVOID SETTING UP CAMP WITH YOUR INNER CRITIC

It's possible that reading the last chapter brought up some criticism about power words and the point of them. Manifesting doesn't feel like a good fit for everyone. Although Perfectioneurs can find themselves being judgmental or critical of others, their inner critic is much more vicious. Have you seen the viral video of the best friends saying the things they say to themselves out loud and directed towards their friend? Let's just say it is both painful and powerful to recognize how ruthless we can be when criticizing ourselves.

Criticism is part of being human. My inner critic had a field day with trying to determine if my professionalism would be questioned in having a chapter on *inner boss bitch* in this book! The key is to not set up camp with your inner critic. To avoid kicking yourself into a deep, dark hole of judgement and negativity about yourself or preparing to linger there. To prevent cohabiting with criticism for an undetermined amount of time. Remember how Perfectioneurs have strong connections between negative core beliefs and their self-worth? Imagine staying in that visceral, vulnerable place for long periods. It is unpleasant. It is uncomfortable. It is unhelpful to improving mental health.

How do you know you've officially set up camp with criticism? The therapeutic term is catastrophizing. Looking through the lens of negativity and engaging in black and white or all-or-nothing thinking. The *Chicken-Little-sky-is-falling* phenomenon. What thoughts rear their ugly heads? You may find yourself saying that you might as well quit, it's too hard anyways. That your efforts won't matter. That it's out of your control so you can end it now and reduce the hurt or fear of failure in the future.

My inner critic sounds and operates similarly. She likes to go into an all-or-nothing headspace where when the going gets tough, she questions if it's worth it. She tells me, if everything feels like effort, I'm not doing it right. She encourages pivoting and running away from hardship. She feeds feelings of resentment and helplessness. She fixates on control and dysregulates my mood.

Does this sound relatable? Your inner critic might have shown up in Chapter 13 regarding power words and manifesting good things. Perhaps your inner critic doesn't believe in the power of naming and owning something by speaking it out loud. The irony is that by owning our inner critic's existence, getting up close and personal with our patterns of self-sabotage, and making friends with our critical side can actually disarm it.

When you close your eyes and allow yourself to feel your inner critic, what does it look like? Are they a person or an object? My inner critic looks like a gigantic thumb pushing me down, trying to

## CHAPTER 14 - AVOID SETTING UP CAMP WITH YOUR INNER CRITIC

squish me like a bug. Once you identify what your inner critic looks like, can you talk to it as if it's a separate entity to help reduce its power? Do you notice when it likes to show up? Understanding the purpose and patterns of self-doubt can be the meaningful strategy to avoid setting up camp with criticism or allowing it to rule over you.

### *Perfectioneur Pointers:* CRITIC IS AS CRITIC DOES

- ★ When you close your eyes, what does your inner critic look like?

- ★ What patterns do you notice about your inner critic? Certain themes to what they say? Specific times they like to show up?

- ★ What can you say to yourself to reduce your inner critic's power? How can you contain that inner voice so it can't rule your emotions and behaviors?

# 15
# LEARNING TO ACCEPT COMPLIMENTS

Finding things to say to yourself to disarm your inner critic can be challenging, to say the least. As humans, we have established we are hardest on and most critical of ourselves. Perfectioneurs take this to another level by endorsing the *shoulds* at all times. The belief that they *should* be hard working. They *should* accomplish their goals. They *should* excel in their plans for the future. In order to squash the self-critic as the enforcer of the *shoulds*, Perfectioneurs must train themselves to accept compliments.

I know, I know, your inner critic just screamed bloody murder inside your head that this puts you at risk of being seen as superficial and cocky. The opposite of humble. That it makes you a jerk. I'm not saying you should fish for compliments, that's just not your style. Instead, I'm asking you to consider allowing yourself to sit with compliments. Perfectioneurs have mastered the automatic thank you and redirect, the thank you and move on, the thank-you-with-uncomfortable-chuckle-and-change-of-subject strategy. Consider the power of pausing to take it in. To notice what feelings come up when receiving a compliment. To experience any pleasant sensations. To remain present.

In therapy, this is a focus of self-esteem and growth goals. So many young adults find themselves uncomfortable with compliments. Even in the office as a place of safety, they smile and fidget. They redirect the conversation as quickly as possible. Their body rejects the compliment with some throw-away gesture or shrug that prevents it from absorbing below the surface. *Water off a duck's back.* Why would I ask them, and you, to pause and take it in? Because it reinforces pleasant sensations of pride, joy, and excitement. *Or* it gives us something to work on therapeutically when you feel the sensations of discomfort, avoidance, and anxiety instead.

My inner critic, keeper of the *shoulds*, struggles to take compliments not only from a place of accomplishments or hard work being *expected* but also from a place of caution. As an Enneagram Type 3 Wing 2, my accomplishments and image seen by others matters to me. I hold myself to high standards of accomplishment and am constantly looking to the next goal or task. The caution lies in not wanting to be seen as egotistical or superficial. To avoid steamrolling others. To be seen instead as influential and impactful.

My clients take caution to another level when they share that compliments come with a cost. From the place of trauma, clients wonder what strings are attached, what the person wants in return, or what manipulation is afoot. Having experienced significant or repeat relational trauma, their brains prevent them from taking a compliment to heart. It can be seen as both heartbreaking and

## CHAPTER 15 - LEARNING TO ACCEPT COMPLIMENTS

self-preserving. Therefore training ourselves to accept compliments is a process, and requires patience and presence to allow any feelings to be observed and absorbed.

## *Perfectioneur Pointers*: PRESENCE WITH COMPLIMENTS

★ Practice pausing for 2-3 seconds after receiving a compliment. Notice what sensations appear. Follow up by looking the other person in the eye and saying thank you.

★ Allow yourself some stillness when receiving a compliment. Notice any fidgeting or nervous gestures that come up and identify ways to express them through movement after the exchange.

★ Once you've gotten past the discomfort of compliments, take #1 a step further by elaborating on your thank you and articulating what receiving the compliment means for you. For example, "thank you, that means so much to me." "Thank you, I appreciate it." "Thank you, that reassures me that I'm on the right track." "Thank you, I love these shoes too!" "Thank you for noticing."

# 16
# LEAN INTO LEADERSHIP

By training yourself to accept compliments, you learn to be more present and aware. This helps you lean into leadership roles within your career and community by showing up as authentic and trustworthy. A magical combination for impact and contribution in the workforce. As Perfectioneurs continue to kick ass and develop a reputation for getting things done, it's not uncommon for them to be promoted or recruited into leadership roles. They may even pursue a leadership role themselves in seeing it as aligned with their goals.

As I began my wellness journey as a Perfectioneur, I learned that my leadership style needed some work. I initially showed up as a driving force, setting performance measures for myself and others, identifying fast-paced deadlines that added unwanted pressure, and finding myself frustrated when goals took longer to be achieved. In my most unhealthy form, I lost my ability to be pleasant and sympathetic to life factors that added to delays. Leadership calls for collaboration and communication to get things done, including a level of commitment and dependability that encourages others to sign on to your vision and mission. My team reports they have always felt that I had their backs and would go to bat for them, but it is only in recent years that I've successfully slowed down in wanting to build a more heart-felt connection with each of them to support their goals and dreams within the business.

Do you find yourself called to leadership to support impact and meaning? Have you invested in any leadership trainings to support self-discovery and added insight? I have to admit, I am a leadership training addict. Every time I engage in a training, I discover new things about myself and truly invest in the time to do deeper work! I hope you too can embrace opportunities in leadership to contribute to the bigger picture within your workplace and community. Leadership can support your values as well as provide opportunities for ongoing contributions towards meaningful change.

## *Perfectioneur Pointers*: LESSONS IN LEADERSHIP

- ★ Perfectioneurs are naturally considered for leadership roles in their reputation of achieving results.

- ★ Explore leadership resources to continue to grow both personally and professionally.

- ★ Invest in leadership training as time carved out to do deeper work.

# 17
# THE POWER OF VULNERABILITY

Our *Spidey sense* reminds us that with great leadership comes great responsibility. Er, something like that. Simon Sinek (2019) is one game-changer in the leadership conversation who reiterates that successful leaders create infinite mindsets and facilitate powerful change. Many professionals emphasize leadership as dynamic and powerful, leading to well-known concepts such as *actions speaking louder than words* and *leading by example*. What if I told you that leadership is also about vulnerability?

For some Perfectioneurs that are reading this book, you again had a reaction. Perhaps it was nervousness, anxiety, or sheer panic. I know for myself, identifying as a Perfectioneur initially meant striving for perfection and avoiding failure. Vulnerability feels like the gateway to failure in that it feels risky, like we are exposed, standing naked in front of our most influential and valued colleagues. To quote *A Knight's Tale (2001)*, "you have been weighed, you have been measured, and you have been found wanting." How can that not invite panic and your inner critic to the party? I had vulnerability drilled into me as part of my wellness plan, my resistance met with the reminder that I am in fact human and may have vulnerable moments show up without my consent. I was also reminded that when my vulnerability has appeared in the past, the world did not end as the result.

So how does one embrace vulnerability? By using it to tell our story. Brené Brown (2015) is the champion of vulnerability leading to meaningful connections and outcomes. I decided to put vulnerability to the test in front of 50 entrepreneurs. 50 business owners who were forces to be reckoned with in their own fields. My imposter syndrome had shown up, calling myself a fraud and feeling intimidated by their successes and their years in business. Pointing out my younger age and limited experience. Yet I knew I needed to tap into the emotion of my story, as we'd all been assigned to present 3-minute pitches to highlight growth opportunities within our business. How could my pitch not be emotional when it focused on mental health and suicide prevention?

The vulnerability I embraced was sharing my story as a suicide loss survivor and resulting passion for suicide prevention. Vulnerability was allowing emotion to show in my voice as it wavered and not swallowing it or shoving it down. It was embracing the power of my words and allowing myself to feel each of them as I spoke them out loud. It was being unapologetic that I was shaking on the inside while standing tall on the outside. And it was asking for their help through a powerful call to action. The result? A standing ovation, a check written on the spot by a fellow entrepreneur to support the cause, and an opportunity to do it again in front of 100 entrepreneurs the next day, winning a pitch competition that facilitated greater exposure as a business. It was amazing. It was exhilarating. It was exhausting. I was emotionally and physically drained afterwards, keyed up and jittery, unable to sit still. The power of vulnerability allowed me to show up more authentically than I had ever before, and I survived! It was positive! It was productive! It proved worthwhile!

How can you embrace your own vulnerability? Where can you practice telling your story? What are ways it can feel worthwhile for you? For Perfectioneurs, I know this is a big ask. It takes practice, like many of the concepts in this book. I assure you, it is one area that truly feels life-changing once it's embraced. People will be drawn to you because of your vulnerability and authenticity. For those called to make a meaningful change or impact, vulnerability is an important part of the larger equation.

## *Perfectioneur Pointers*: VULNERABILITY IS VALUED

- ★ Vulnerability is authenticity.
- ★ Vulnerability is telling your story.
- ★ Where can you practice vulnerability in your life?

# 18
# ASKING FOR HELP

Vulnerability facilitates connection through authentic communication and story-telling. Perfectioneurs are drawn to leadership roles as an opportunity to have a bigger ripple effect, and with that comes increased responsibility. So how does this impact work-life balance and the idea of self-care? For many, it brings us to the second example of vulnerability which is asking for help.

Remember how we identified Perfectioneurs as having negative core beliefs tied to self-worth? How they view vulnerability initially as weakness or failure? How they might pursue leadership to make a greater difference in the world? Well we also know that it takes more than one person to catalyze change. *It takes a movement.* It takes teamwork. Asking for help becomes an essential element in delegating tasks and supporting progress. The ego of an unhealthy Perfectioneur says that we should do it ourselves. To get it done right, we have to do it on our own. Yet any business strategist will tell you it's more about the team backing a great leader than it is the leader themselves. Professional pitches and investors are focusing on team dynamics and representation as a measurement of potential business success (Grant, 2017). Why wouldn't we explore the same?

I learned this the hard way myself when entering the nonprofit sector. I'd done all the research, investing time and energy into taking coursework to better understand the structure. I'd set up a framework to get the nonprofit off the ground in the first year, hosting two successful community events, obtaining private donations, and obtaining our first community grant. I'd recruited amazing professionals with a passion for mental health and suicide prevention to serve on the Board. *But I had made a mistake.* I made the mistake of asking the Board members to commit to one year to help me get it up and running. What was I thinking?! My Perfectioneur brain said we could accomplish all we needed to in that first year, that the timeline was reasonable. Not surprising, my timeline was off once again and Board members started to exit, having served the term I'd asked of them.

Fast forward to the year and a half mark of the nonprofit's existence and I was drowning in responsibility. I was trying to run three businesses simultaneously and I found old habits trying to creep their way back in. Habits of working weekends, not taking breaks to walk, and forgoing balanced, sit-down meals for items on my agenda. I needed help and I needed to embrace my vulnerability to ask for it. With some nerves, I found myself on a video call with the Board and did my best to remain grounded, assertive, and heartfelt. I named the challenges and asked for their help. Their responses were favorable. We were able to repair any feelings they had of being

## CHAPTER 18 - ASKING FOR HELP

obsolete in my drive to see results, and I was able to slow down and ask for help in concrete ways they could meet.

Where have you needed to ask for help? How did you approach it? Asking for help isn't about weakness, it's about strength. Remembering strength is within the bigger picture of results and finding the strength to get out of our own way. Asking for help can support the work-life balance we all crave by not assuming we can or *should* do it all. The assumption of being able to do it all is what puts us a greatest risk of relapse as a healthy Perfectioneur.

### *Perfectioneur Pointers:* ASKING CREATES SPACE FOR SELF-CARE

- ★ Asking for help is a strength.

- ★ Asking for help frees up time for self-care and work-life balance strategies.

- ★ What are two ways you can ask for help when you need it? Who would you ask?

# 19
# THE RISK OF RELAPSE

Relapse is a charged word. A sometimes scary word. A word for sliding backwards in progress. In the case of Perfectioneurs, relapse can describe the subtle shifts of old habits resurfacing or the landslide into workaholic status. The landslide is easier to notice. Yet for many Perfectioneurs, it starts off more subtle. Perhaps its saying yes to a project even though you want to say no. Maybe it's that twinge of regret when realizing that a current project has lost direction and doesn't feel like it serves you, but you ignore it and push through anyway. *After all, you've come this far right?* What if relapse shows up in longer work days, working weekends, forgetting to eat, or forgoing exercise for one more call or series of emails? What if it shows up because you don't want to disappoint others?

Truthfully, my relapse warning signs look like all of the above and more. The subtle ones creep up and if I'm stuck in a desire for progress or momentum, I don't always notice or acknowledge them. Sometimes it takes someone I value or trust to call me on my crap. A client of mine in AA shared the importance of identifying someone "who doesn't co-sign your bullshit." I love this idea! In fact, I asked two colleagues I know and respect if they could be my people for that very purpose. Outside of coaches who will absolutely point out patterns from a place of rapport and respect, I needed colleagues who see me in my element day-to-day to check me. I needed people I trusted to tell me how it is and help me shift away from unhealthy patterns. People I knew wouldn't let me pave my own way to steamrolling over others. People who've seen me at my best, my worst, excited, and exhausted. I'm lucky to have them.

Who comes to mind for you? Who can be your relapse prevention person? Your accountability buddy? Your fellow entrepreneur or Perfectioneur pursuing work-life balance? Are you aware of your warning signs for emotional, physical, and relational decline? Do you have a plan in place to get back on track if you start to slide? With clients, I value the benefits of handwritten goals and plans to help them get back on track. Developing visuals of their functioning and next steps to pursue wellness while accessing resources and supports that fulfill the need that's coming up. There's something powerful about the brain-body connection when writing out ideas or journaling. I encourage you to try it as part of your relapse prevention plan.

## *Perfectioneur Pointers*: RELAPSE PREVENTION PLANNING

- ★ Think about your warning signs for relapse. If you get stuck, ask your loved ones what they see in you when you are stressed.

## CHAPTER 19 - THE RISK OF RELAPSE

★ Who can be your accountability buddy when things need to change? Who will tell you how it is and help you shift gears?

★ Write down your warning signs and a plan of action to get back to recovery. What themes come up? What plans could work for you?

# 20
# REST VERSUS RESTORATION

Planning ways to stay in recovery is a crucial piece of the work-life balance we all aspire to and want for our busy lives. Self-care has been mentioned before in this book as a strategy to stay balanced. The difficulty with self-care is that it's been commercialized. Clients experiencing financial difficulties or poverty communicate that they feel like they cannot *afford* self-care. When digging deeper, we learn that many people believe self-care to be manicures/pedicures, vacations, spa days, massages, and more. From this limiting lens, we can begin to better understand why people aren't engaging in self-care consistently in ways that feel helpful.

Please allow me to reframe self-care as the concept of *rest versus restoration*. Rest is the idea of allowing the body and mind to slow down. For some young adult Americans, this is the don't-get-dressed-stay-in-pjs-all-weekend phenomenon. The idea of binge-watching a show, sleeping in, ordering take-out, and not leaving the house. Yet some of these same young adults come to therapy during the week and report they still feel fatigued, exhausted, or unmotivated. They claim that resting didn't help them bounce back like they had hoped. *Enter restoration*. Restoration can be defined as the things that energize us. Things that light us up, that revitalize us. When framed from this perspective, the list of self-care items or ideas changes. Perhaps now the list is about engaging in activities that bring pleasure and lightness, like dancing, music, cooking, and nature. Maybe it's spending time with certain individuals that energize us and encourage playfulness or creativity. It's amazing and reassuring to see that many restorative activities don't feel extravagant or costly, making them more accessible to everyone.

I know now that restorative for me means surrounding myself with creative entrepreneurs, family, and nature. It's walking daily and making sure I move throughout the day. It's ensuring I get my 8-9 hours of sleep each night and get up the same time every day. For Perfectioneurs, restorative activities aren't always easy to embrace. They are the first things sacrificed to workaholic tendencies, removed from agendas to make room for other projects or deadlines. They are the things that suffer when Perfectioneurs succumb to burnout and fatigue. They are the things lost to the illusion of progress and momentum. Therefore restorative activities are even more critical to maintain and schedule into your routine weekly, if not daily. What first drew me to my coach on the journey of recovery as a Perfectioneur was her honesty that self-care didn't come easy to her. I could relate to that and value her statements that self-care can suck because it requires effort and practice. Allow yourself to notice what

## CHAPTER 20 - REST VERSUS RESTORATION

revitalizes you and make note to do it more. Pinpoint when you need rest versus restoration to feel your best. Understand that self-care takes practice, it is not easy or effortless. However you approach it, I'm confident it will be the reframe needed to be more successful with your self-care, creating new habits that feel worthwhile in your everyday routine.

### *Perfectioneur Pointers*: SELF-CARE REDEFINED

- ★ Write down some examples of things that create rest vs. restoration for you.
- ★ Explore what gets in the way of your self-care.
- ★ Identify one area of self-care to focus on for the week and notice what shifts for you as the result.

# 21
# WATCH YOUR WARNING SIGNS

We want to feel restored. We want to feel balanced and energized. *What happens when everything feels like effort, even self-care?* I can definitely relate to the feeling that trying to take care of myself feels like a lot of work. Self-care is difficult for small business owners and Perfectioneurs because it takes effort to schedule it and follow through! The influence of workaholic culture combined with growing burnout risks requires creativity to combat the resulting fatigue. Which means watching out for warning signs or a sudden plummet in workaholism becomes even more critical when striving for health and wellness as Perfectioneurs.

So what are we tracking? In addition to the 40+ symptoms of burnout listed in the companion Perfectioneur Workbook, now we are looking at the social impact of fatigue. Extroverts are feeling lonely and unhappy in not getting quality time with others. Introverts are feeling even more drained from shorter spells of interaction.

I know that for me, social isolation has contributed to a recent relapse into workaholism in wanting to feel in control of something. I wanted to feel like I was progressing even when I couldn't control the world around me. To reject the uncertainty and ignore the unknown. To bury feelings of anxiety and stagnation. It's natural that as humans, we want to avoid pain. Instead, I threw myself into projects and productivity. As a self-identified control freak, this reaction doesn't surprise me at all. What has surprised me is how we've all had to tap into our creativity once again to find joy in the little things to keep burnout at bay.

So what can we embrace in our routines that unlock feelings of pleasure and restoration without draining our energy supply in the face of fatigue? Perhaps the activities you choose to do solo look different than the activities you'd like to do with others. Revisiting *who's in your orbit*, it's possible you've pinpointed who you'd like to spend time with and why. Once you've identified the people in your life who can invest in joy with you, the next step is to explore both passive and active interactions that can feel energizing. Perhaps it's listening to music together or taking a drive to passively recharge. Maybe it's a joint exercise class or playing games in a more active interaction. Consider the activities you value doing alone as an opportunity to rest versus the things you'd like to do with others to recharge and make time for both of them!

## *Perfectioneur Pointers*: WINNING IN WELLNESS

★ Identify both passive and active self-care strategies to reduce burnout.

## CHAPTER 21 - WATCH YOUR WARNING SIGNS

★ Explore activities you can enjoy by yourself to recharge against workaholism.

★ Discover restorative self-care with others and schedule it, or it won't happen.

# 22
# SAY YES TO NO (MORE)!

Part of reducing your warning signs for workaholism is learning to say no. No to working your weekends. No to longer hours. No to working for free. A fellow professional describes it as *acting your wage*. As in, you work the hours that you are paid to work. But how does this apply to driven Perfectioneurs as our own bosses? Where no one tells us what to work on and when? Where our vision and purpose cause us to blur the boundaries in order to discover momentum and success?

I'll be the first to admit to backsliding into workaholism when I'm not careful with my boundaries. It's happened to me multiple times! The usual culprits? The enthusiasm of new projects. The anxiety of saying no and disappointing others. The flattery of them asking me for help. That familiar worry of a missed opportunity. It takes conscious effort to catch ourselves before we backslide into old habits. It's a balancing act to say yes to no more.

How would you respond to the following questions?

"Can I pick your brain?"

"I have this project I think you'd love. Can we find a time to connect on it?"

"I need your help."

"What's your availability this week?"

As you build your reputation and brand as a passionate entrepreneur, more and more people will come out of the woodwork asking for your help or contribution on their projects. The value is in feeling prepared for when these requests land in your inbox. How can you respond in ways that honor your values and boundaries without burning bridges for future collaboration?

I suggest having some drafted responses that reduce your anxiety when saying no. For example:

"Thanks for asking! I'm working on some time-sensitive projects right now and have included my calendar of availability to schedule next month if you'd like."

"Hello! I can't commit to a new project until _____. Would you like to reconnect then?"

Some entrepreneurs and coaches say you aren't obligated to respond at all. That suggestion goes against my values and work ethic, so I've discovered that having some set responses that sound genuine and authentic serve me better. People assume that you are busy. *You are.* Timing is critical when accomplishing the goals you've set for yourself with minimal distractions. Remember that your top 10 goals are your priority! Therefore, taking the time to craft your responses and keeping them handy can reduce any anxiety that shows up when saying no to more.

## CHAPTER 22 - SAY YES TO NO (MORE)!

### *Perfectioneur Pointers:* NO MORE RIGHT NOW

- ★ Strengthen your ability to say no by revisiting your top ten goals.

- ★ Recognize that the person asking for help is prepared for no to be your answer.

- ★ Find your voice in crafting no-thank-you responses to make the process easier on you both.

# 23
# FIND YOUR VOICE

Notice all the shifts that can take place as you work towards your healthiest self as a Perfectioneur. If this isn't you, perhaps you are attempting to help a Perfectioneur in your life. The journey is full of twists and turns as we embrace our strengths, challenges, and next steps to achieve a more balanced, impactful life. The positive shifts aren't always in-your-face noticeable. Sometimes it comes from someone you know who makes a comment that you seem more relaxed and present. Perhaps it's the colleague who reports they don't feel your anxiety anymore when they walk past your desk. Maybe it's the family member who shares how happy they are to see you more often now that you've changed up your schedule, or the friend who looks forward to coffee with you each month knowing you won't cancel because you made another commitment.

I can admit amusement with myself that I started my recovery journey balking at the idea of taking a 10 minute walking break each day. Recognizing the resistance until I saw the benefits and now it's part of my everyday agenda. It is no longer an effort; it is a habit. It is one of the most enjoyable parts of my day. It's something my Perfectioneur brain initially resisted in "not having enough time." Some psychologists and coaches say we make time for the things that matter. This matters, so I continue to make time and reap the benefits.

An even more significant shift came from the observations of others regarding my leadership and communication. By embracing authenticity and vulnerability, I've found that I command more from my colleagues in ways that are both collaborative and empowering. My coach says I've found my voice. It's a voice she describes as more self-assured, honest, and confident. It's defined in how I carry myself, how I speak, and how I show up on video or speaking in public. It's defined by my joy at family dinners and walks with my sister. It's the freedom of having an unplanned day with my spouse. It's the pleasure of having blank space on my calendar for creativity.

My hope as a therapist and fellow entrepreneur is that you will find your voice by embracing the good, the bad, and the ugly of being a Perfectioneur. You too can discover your authentic, entrepreneurial self. I'm proud to be a Perfectioneur with all my edges and my strengths. I'm privileged to work with other entrepreneurs and young adults trying to leave their mark in this world without burning out. I'm honored to engage others on the very things I too need to continue to work on, so that we may all show up as our best selves.

★ Remove the badge of busyness.

★ Embrace vulnerability and ask for help.

## CHAPTER 23 - FIND YOUR VOICE

- ★ Rediscover joy in the face of fatigue.

- ★ *To conquer or die* no longer applies.

You know now that you too can be successful without running yourself into the ground. *I see you.* We are in this together. With these tools and your Perfectioneur spirit, work-life balance will be more reachable and rewarding than you previously thought possible. Get out there and truly live!

# HOST A *TYPE A SOIREE*

Ready for National Book Month? Want to bring friends and driven professionals together? Check out the activities below for your next book club and dive right in!

## Balance Over Burnout Book Club

1. Why do you think perfectionism is on the rise?

2. Do you relate to Perfectioneurs? Why or why not?

3. What's your biggest takeaway from *Perfectioneur*?

4. What are some ideas to reduce contact with negative influences (from Chapter 11: Who's in Your Orbit)?

5. What's one thing you've shifted or changed since reading *Perfectioneur*?

6. What's one thing you still want to change? How can the group support you?

## A Deeper Dive with these Downloads

- Go Lean on Lists with Your Book Buddies (Exercise 7)

- NEW! Watch Your Warning Signs (Exercise 21)

- NEW! Say Yes to No (More)! Explore Scripts for Saying No (Exercise 22)

**Grab the Perfectioneur Workbook for all 22 exercises at perfectioneur.com.**

## Battle Burnout Culture with these Recommended Readings

- *Burnout: The Secret to Unlocking the Stress Cycle* by Emily Nagoski and Amelia Nagoski

- *Can't Even: How Millennials Became the Burnout Generation* by Anne Helen Petersen

- *Do Nothing: How to Break Away from Overworking, Overdoing, and Underliving* by Celeste Headlee

- *Trauma Stewardship: An Everyday Guide to Caring for Self While Caring for Others* by Laura van Dernoot Lipsky and Connie Burk

# REFERENCES

Brown, B. (2015). *Daring greatly: How the courage to be vulnerable transforms the way we live, love, parent, and lead.* Avery.

Debczak, M. (2019, December 6). *Revised guidelines redefine birth years and classifications for Gen X, Millennials, and Gen Z.* Mentalfloss. https://www.mentalfloss.com/article/609811/age-ranges-millennials-and-generation-z

Drexler, P. (2019, March 1). Millennials are the therapy generation. Wall Street Journal, https://www.wsj.com/articles/millennials-are-the-therapy-generation-11551452286

Freeman, M., Johnson, S., Staudenmaier, P., & Zisser, M. (2015). *Are entrepreneurs touched with fire?* http://www.michaelafreemanmd.com/Research_files/Are%20Entrepreneurs%20Touched%20with%20Fire%20(pre-pub%20n)%204-17-15.pdf

Grant, A. (2017). *Originals: How non-conformists move the world.* Penguin Books.

Riso, D.R. & Hudson, R. (1996). *Personality types: using the enneagram for self-discovery.* Mariner Books.

Shapiro, F. (2001). *Eye movement desensitization and reprocessing (EMDR): Basic principles, protocols, and procedures,* 2nd edition. The Guilford Press.

Shlesinger, I. (2018). *Elder Millennial.* Netflix Standup Comedy Special. https://www.youtube.com/watch?v=CWsJPr3ML4M

Sinek, S. (2009). *Start with why: how great leaders inspire everyone to take action.* New York: Portfolio.

Twenge, J.M. (2017). *IGen: why today's super-connected kids are growing up less rebellious, more tolerant, less happy—and completely unprepared for adulthood (and what this means for the rest of us).* First Atria books hardcover edition. New York, NY: Atria Books.

www.ingramcontent.com/pod-product-compliance
Lightning Source LLC
Chambersburg PA
CBHW050241220526
45465CB00002B/509